GOD HAS SET BEFORE YOU AN OPEN DOOR

Embracing and Maximizing the Promises of God

Pastor Dr. Claudine Benjamin

Published by:

Editor: Cleveland O. McLeish (Author C. Orville McLeish)

ISBN: 978-1-965635-50-6 (paperback)

Dedication

To every believer standing before a threshold of change—this book is dedicated to you.

To the one who has waited, wrestled, prayed, and wondered if the door would ever open.

To the one who has felt unqualified, unnoticed, or unsure.

To the one who has dared to believe again after disappointment.

May you find the courage to walk through every door God sets before you.

May you discover that His timing is perfect, His purpose is unstoppable, and His presence goes before you.

This book is for you—because your door is open. Walk in.

And above all, to the One who opens and no one can shut—Jesus Christ, my Savior, my Door, and my Shepherd. To Him be all the glory.

Acknowledgment

First and foremost, I give all honor and glory to God, the Door-Opener, the Promise-Keeper, and the Author of my destiny. Without His voice, Spirit, and faithfulness, this message would not exist. Thank You, Lord, for every season of waiting, every lesson in obedience, and every open door that brought me closer to You.

To my family—thank you for being my foundation, strength, and constant support. Your love and encouragement continue to push me forward when I feel like turning back.

To my spiritual leaders, mentors, and friends who prayed for me, corrected me, and believed in me—thank you for helping me discern and walk through the doors God set before me.

To every reader who picks up this book—thank you for trusting me to speak into your life. I pray that every page pushes you closer to God's purpose and ignites your boldness to step into your next season.

Lastly, to those who've gone before, paved the way, or stood at their own doors with trembling faith—your legacy lives on in the obedience of others. Thank you.

About the Author

Pastor Claudine Benjamin is a passionate preacher, teacher, and writer with a prophetic voice for this generation. Known for her heartfelt messages, biblical depth, and commitment to the gospel of Jesus Christ, she ministers with boldness, compassion, and clarity. Her mandate is to awaken the body of Christ to its divine purpose and to stir hearts toward obedience, revival, and the urgent call of God.

With years of pastoral and evangelistic experience, Pastor Claudine is no stranger to storms, seasons of waiting, or the weight of divine assignments. Through each trial and triumph, she has come to know firsthand the power of walking through the doors that God opens— doors of healing, calling, restoration, and destiny.

In *God Has Set Before You an Open Door,* she writes not from theory but from lived encounters with the faithfulness of God. Her voice resounds with encouragement to those who feel shut out, held back, or forgotten. She reminds readers that when God opens a door, no man can shut it (see **Revelation 3:8**).

Pastor Claudine continues to write books that uplift, equip, and challenge the believer to walk in their God-given purpose. Her works reflect her deep burden for soul-winning, discipleship, spiritual growth, and kingdom advancement.

When she is not writing or ministering, she mentors others, leads prayer gatherings, and empowers the next generation to rise up and fulfill their calling. She is a firm believer that purpose cannot be buried, destiny cannot be denied, and no closed door can cancel what God has ordained.

Table of Contents

Introduction

The Power of the Open Door

"I know your deeds. See, I have placed before you an open door that no one can shut." —Revelation 3:8a (NIV)

A Divine Invitation

In the bustling city of Philadelphia, amidst the challenges and trials faced by early Christians, Jesus extends a profound promise: an open door that no one can shut. This declaration is not merely a statement of opportunity but a testament to divine authority and favor. It signifies access to God's kingdom, the assurance of His presence, and the unfolding of His divine plan in our lives.

The Key of David: Authority and Access

The imagery of the "key of David" in **Revelation 3:7** harks back to **Isaiah 22:22**, where Eliakim is entrusted with the key to the house of David, symbolizing authority and governance. In the context of Revelation, this key represents Jesus' sovereign authority over the kingdom of God. He opens doors of opportunity, salvation, and service that no one can close, and He closes doors that no one can open. This authority assures believers that the pathways He establishes are secure and divinely ordained.

Embracing the Open Door

The concept of an open door is multifaceted, encompassing opportunities for evangelism, spiritual growth, and deeper communion with God. In **Acts 14:27**, Paul speaks of God opening a door of faith to the Gentiles, highlighting the expansion of the gospel. Similarly, in **1 Corinthians 16:9**, he refers to a great door for effective work that has been opened to him. These passages illustrate that open doors are divine invitations to participate in God's redemptive work.

A Call to Faithfulness

The church in Philadelphia is commended for its faithfulness despite having "little strength." Their steadfastness in keeping God's Word and not denying His name positioned them to receive this promise of an open door. It serves as a reminder that God's opportunities are not reserved for the strong or influential but are extended to those who remain faithful and obedient.

Walking Through the Door

Recognizing an open door is the first step; choosing to walk through it requires faith and courage. It involves trusting in God's timing, embracing His calling, and stepping into the unknown with confidence in His guidance.

As we journey through this book, we will explore the various dimensions of God's open doors, learn how to discern them, and discover how to navigate the paths they lead us on. May this exploration inspire you to recognize and embrace the open doors God sets before you, leading to a deeper relationship with Him and a more profound impact in His kingdom.

Chapter 1

He Holds the Keys

The Authority of the Key

In the ancient Near East, keys were not merely tools for locking and unlocking doors; they symbolized authority and trust. When a king entrusted someone with a key, it signified granting them control over access to the royal household and its treasures. This imagery is vividly portrayed in **Isaiah 22:22**, where God declares: **"I will place on his shoulder the key to the house of David; what he opens no one can shut, and what he shuts no one can open." (NIV).**

This passage refers to Eliakim, who was appointed as the steward over King Hezekiah's household, replacing the unfaithful Shebna. The "key to the house of David" symbolizes the authority bestowed upon Eliakim to govern and make decisions on behalf of the king.

Jesus: The Ultimate Key Holder

Fast forward to the New Testament, and we see this imagery applied to Jesus Christ in **Revelation 3:7: "To the angel of the church in Philadelphia write: These are the words of him who is holy and true, who holds the key of David. What he opens no one can shut, and what he shuts no one can open." (NIV).**

Here, Jesus is depicted as the one who holds ultimate authority over the kingdom of God. The "key of David" signifies His sovereign power to grant or deny access to God's kingdom, blessings, and purposes. Unlike Eliakim, whose authority was limited to the earthly kingdom of Judah, Jesus' authority is eternal and encompasses all of creation.

The Open Door Set Before Us

In **Revelation 3:8a**, Jesus continues His message to the church in Philadelphia: **"I know your deeds. See, I have placed before you an open door that no one can shut."**

This "open door" represents opportunities for ministry, spiritual growth, and access to God's presence. It is a door that Jesus Himself has opened, and no human or spiritual force can close it. This assurance is especially comforting for believers facing opposition, persecution, or feelings of inadequacy.

Trusting in His Sovereignty

Understanding that Jesus holds the keys should instill confidence in us. He opens doors that lead to life, purpose, and fulfillment, and He closes doors that may lead to harm or distraction. Our role is to trust in His wisdom and timing, seeking His guidance in every decision and step we take.

Reflective Questions

1. Are there areas in your life where you need to trust Jesus' authority to open or close doors?

2. How can you align your actions with the opportunities He sets before you?

3. In what ways can you encourage others to recognize and walk through the open doors Jesus provides?

Declaration

I declare that Jesus Christ holds the keys of authority over my life, my destiny, and every door that leads to His perfect will. I trust in His sovereign wisdom to open what no man can shut and to shut what no man can open. I will not fear missed opportunities, rejection, or delay—for my times are in His hands. I walk boldly through the open doors He has set before me, knowing they lead to life, purpose, and eternal significance. Where He leads, I will follow. What He closes, I will release. In all things, I rest in the truth that He is faithful, holy, and true—my Keeper, my Guide, and the One who holds the keys.

Prayer

Lord Jesus, thank You for holding the keys to every door in our lives. Help us to trust in Your sovereignty, to recognize the doors You open, and to walk through them with faith and obedience. Close the doors that are not in alignment with Your will, and guide us in the path You have set before us. Amen.

Chapter 2

The Promise to Philadelphia

"I know thy works: behold, I have set before thee an open door, and no man can shut it…" —Revelation 3:8a (KJV)

A Church with Little Strength but Great Faith

The church in Philadelphia was not known for its size, wealth, or influence. In fact, Jesus acknowledged that they had "little strength" **(see Revelation 3:8)**. Yet, what they did possess was infinitely more valuable in God's eyes: faithfulness.

They were not praised for perfection or prominence, but for perseverance. This ancient city, renowned for its earthquakes and instability, was home to believers who remained steadfast in their faith, grounded in God's Word, and unwavering in their commitment to His name. They didn't deny Him in trials, and as a result, Jesus offered them a breathtaking promise: an open door that no man could shut.

What Does the Open Door Represent?

The "open door" in **Revelation 3:8** symbolizes more than just opportunity. It represents:

- Access to divine favor.
- Spiritual advancement.
- Opportunity for ministry.

- Kingdom responsibility.
- Protection and reward.

Jesus is not merely offering a chance; He is extending an invitation to walk in divine purpose. This door is not one we open by force or clever strategy—it is opened by the One who holds the key of David.

Scripture Focus

"These are the words of him who is holy and true, who holds the key of David. What he opens no one can shut, and what he shuts no one can open." —Revelation 3:7 (NIV)

Jesus alone has the authority to open doors of destiny. What a comfort this is in a world of gatekeepers, favoritism, and rejection! When man says "no," God can still say "yes." When systems fail, God's door stands wide open.

Faithfulness Over Fame

The believers in Philadelphia weren't noticed for fame or fortune. But heaven noticed their consistency:

- They kept God's Word in a culture of compromise.
- They refused to deny His name when it was inconvenient.
- They didn't use their "little strength" as an excuse—they used it to press in.

Jesus rewarded their faithfulness, not with earthly accolades, but with an eternal open door. This shows that God doesn't require great strength—just great dependence.

Modern Application: What Door Has God Placed Before You?

Many believers today are so focused on what they lack—resources, connections, strength—that they fail to see the open door right in front of them.

The same Jesus who walked among the lampstands and spoke to the churches of Asia Minor is speaking today. If you are remaining faithful, even in weakness, He says to you: *"I have set before you an open door."*

This might be:

- A door of influence in your community.
- A door of reconciliation in your family.
- A door of calling into ministry or a new season.
- A door of healing after years of pain.

No matter the door, if Jesus opened it, no one—not even you—can shut it.

Key Scriptures

- Revelation 3:7–8
- 1 Corinthians 16:9
- Colossians 4:3
- 2 Corinthians 2:12

Reflection

- Have you been measuring your usefulness to God by your strength—or by your faithfulness?

- What opportunities might God be placing before you today that you've overlooked?

- Are you ready to walk through the door He has opened, trusting that He's already gone before you?

Declaration

Jesus, You have placed before me an open door. I choose not to fear, hesitate, or retreat. I will walk through in obedience, faith, and trust, knowing that what You've opened, no man can shut. My strength may be small, but my faith is in You.

Prayer

Lord, help me not to despise the days of small strength. Let me be like the faithful church of Philadelphia—steadfast, obedient, and courageous. Teach me to walk through every door You open with humility and boldness, trusting in Your perfect will. In Jesus' name. Amen.

Chapter 3

Recognizing the Open Door

"See, I have placed before you an open door that no one can shut." —Revelation 3:8 (NIV)

Seeing What God Has Already Set

Many people pray for opportunities, breakthroughs, and favor. But what happens when the door is already open, and we don't recognize it?

God told the church in Philadelphia, **"See, I have set before you an open door."** The command to "see" implies that the door was already there. They weren't being promised something that might come later; they were being asked to discern what God had already provided.

The same applies to you: some doors are not coming—they are already open. The problem isn't opportunity; it's perception.

Spiritual Discernment is Essential

Not every door that looks open is from God, and not every obstacle means the door is closed. That's why we must discern with spiritual eyes, not just with our emotions or logic.

"The person with the Spirit makes judgments about all things…" —1 Corinthians 2:15 (NIV)

God's open doors often require discernment because:

- They may come wrapped in difficulty (see **1 Corinthians 16:9**).
- They may require faith to enter (see **Hebrews 11:8**).
- They may not look the way we expected (see **Isaiah 55:8–9**).

Some people miss God's open doors because they're looking for comfort instead of calling. Others hesitate because the opportunity demands sacrifice, and they assume that if it's hard, it's not God. But divine doors are not always easy—they are always purposeful.

Biblical Examples of Recognizing Open Doors

1. Nehemiah and the Door of Rebuilding

Nehemiah recognized an open door to rebuild the walls of Jerusalem, even though it came with risk and opposition. The king's favor, the burden he felt, and the timing all pointed to God's hand.

"The God of heaven will give us success. We his servants will start rebuilding." —Nehemiah 2:20 (NIV).

2. Paul and the Door for Ministry

Paul often referred to doors being opened by God for his missionary journeys.

"…a great door for effective work has opened to me, and there are many who oppose me." —1 Corinthians 16:9 (NIV).

Notice: the door was open, but the opposition still existed. Opposition does not mean the door is closed. It may actually confirm you're on the right path.

3. Peter's Escape from Prison

When Peter was miraculously released from prison in Acts 12, he didn't initially recognize the open door. He thought he was dreaming!

"Peter came to himself and said, 'Now I know without a doubt that the Lord has sent his angel and rescued me...'" —Acts 12:11 (NIV).

Sometimes, you'll need a moment of awakening to realize that God has already opened the way.

Signs of a God-Opened Door

- It aligns with His Word.
- It draws you closer to Him.
- It requires faith and obedience.
- It blesses others, not just yourself.
- It confirms your calling or assignment.
- It brings peace, even if the path is challenging.

Reflection Questions

1. Are you asking God for doors to open but failing to notice what's already in front of you?

2. Have fear, doubt, or distractions clouded your ability to discern divine opportunities?

3. What are some "small" or "hidden" doors in your life that may actually be significant?

Key Scriptures

- Revelation 3:8
- Isaiah 43:19
- 1 Corinthians 16:9
- Colossians 4:3
- Acts 12:10

Declaration

Lord, give me eyes to see what You have already opened for me. I will not miss my moment of opportunity. I declare that I will walk in discernment, courage, and obedience through every divine door set before me.

Prayer

Father, I ask You to open my eyes to see as You see. Let me not overlook the opportunities You've provided because of fear, familiarity, or doubt. Give me wisdom to recognize Your hand in every area of my life. I surrender my expectations and choose to trust in Your perfect plan. In Jesus' name. Amen.

Chapter 4

Walking by Faith Through the Door

"For we walk by faith, not by sight." —2 Corinthians 5:7 (KJV)

The Door is Open—Now What?

I t's one thing to recognize that a door is open; it's another to walk through it. The door God opens before us often leads into uncharted territory. That's why it requires more than desire—it requires faith.

Faith is the bridge between where you are and where God is calling you to go. The church in Philadelphia had a door set before them, but the text never says they walked through it. Scripture often shows us that it's not enough to have opportunity—we must respond with obedience and courage.

Faith is Not a Feeling

Walking by faith is not walking by comfort or clarity. In fact, many of the doors God opens will challenge our comfort zones and demand a higher level of trust.

"Now faith is the substance of things hoped for, the evidence of things not seen." —Hebrews 11:1 (KJV).

Faith steps forward even when the outcome is not visible. It believes God's Word more than the environment, more than fear, and more than personal limitations.

Example: Abraham

Abraham was called to leave his country and go **"to a land that I will show you"** (see **Genesis 12:1**). He didn't have a road map or a five-year plan. All he had was a word from God—and that was enough.

"By faith Abraham obeyed... and he went out, not knowing where he was going." —Hebrews 11:8 (KJV).

Faith means sometimes walking without knowing, but with full trust that God knows.

Obstacles at the Threshold

When you approach a God-ordained door, you will likely encounter resistance:

- Fear of the unknown.
- Doubt about your ability.
- Voices of discouragement.
- Spiritual warfare.

Just because there's pressure doesn't mean the door is wrong. In fact, the greater the destiny, the greater the resistance. Paul said:

"A great door for effective work has opened to me, and there are many who oppose me." —1 Corinthians 16:9 (NIV).

You Are Not Alone

God doesn't open a door and abandon you on the threshold. He goes before you.

"The Lord himself goes before you and will be with you…" — Deuteronomy 31:8 (NIV).

He provides grace, strength, and direction as you move. Like the priests who carried the Ark of the Covenant into the Jordan River (see **Joshua 3**), the waters didn't part until they put their feet in. Movement activates miracles.

What Keeps People from Walking Through?

- **Analysis paralysis** – Overthinking what's beyond the door.
- **Fear of failure** – Forgetting that God equips whom He calls.
- **Comparison** – Measuring your journey against someone else's.
- **Comfort** – Preferring the familiar over the fruitful.

Faith doesn't guarantee that the journey will be easy, but it guarantees that God will walk it with you.

Faith-Filled Steps to Walk Through

- Pray for courage.
- Remind yourself of God's Word.
- Take the first step, even if it's small.
- Surround yourself with faith-builders.

- Refuse to retreat when it gets uncomfortable.

"The just shall live by faith." —Romans 1:17 (KJV).

Key Scriptures

- 2 Corinthians 5:7
- Hebrews 11:1
- Genesis 12:1–4
- Deuteronomy 31:8
- Joshua 3:13
- Romans 1:17

Reflection Questions

1. What door is God calling you to walk through that feels intimidating?

2. Are you waiting for clarity when God is asking for movement?

3. How can you take one step of faith today?

Declaration

I choose to walk by faith and not by sight. I will not be limited by fear or uncertainty. God has gone before me, and He has made the way. I will move in obedience and trust Him with the outcome.

Prayer

Father, thank You for opening doors in my life. Give me the faith to walk through what You've already prepared. I surrender my fear, my need for control, and my hesitation. I declare that I will trust You more than I trust what I see. Lead me, and I will follow. In Jesus' name, amen.

Chapter 5

Fear Cannot Keep You Out

"For God hath not given us the spirit of fear; but of power, and of love, and of a sound mind." —2 Timothy 1:7 (KJV)

The Door Is Open, But Fear Waits at the Threshold

Fear is one of the most common barriers to stepping into what God has already prepared. The door may be wide open, the invitation extended, the promise confirmed—yet fear still whispers: *"What if it doesn't work?" "What if you fail?" "What if you're not enough?"*

Fear doesn't have to close the door—it only needs to convince you not to walk through it.

God didn't say the church in Philadelphia would have it easy. He said, **"I know you have little strength, yet you have kept my word and not denied my name." (Revelation 3:8 - NIV).** That means they acted in faith despite weakness. That's the very definition of courage: not the absence of fear, but obedience in the presence of it.

Fear Is Not from God

Let's be clear: fear is not a gift from God. Scripture plainly says:

"God hath not given us the spirit of fear..." —2 Timothy 1:7 (KJV).

Fear is a tactic of the enemy—designed to paralyze purpose, shrink vision, and delay destiny. But if fear is not from God, it means we don't have to accept it. We can confront it with the truth of God's Word.

The Three God-Given Replacements for Fear

1. **Power** – Spiritual authority and strength (see Ephesians 3:20).

2. **Love** – God's perfect love that drives out fear (see 1 John 4:18).

3. **A Sound Mind** – Clarity, wisdom, and stability (see Philippians 4:7).

When you operate in these, fear loses its grip.

Biblical Examples of Conquering Fear

1. Joshua: Leading Beyond Fear

God tells Joshua repeatedly to **"be strong and courageous"** (see Joshua 1:9). Why? Because Joshua was stepping into Moses' shoes to lead Israel into the Promised Land. The door was open, but fear threatened to shut it from within.

"Have I not commanded you? Be strong and courageous. Do not be afraid; do not be discouraged, for the Lord your God will be with you wherever you go." —Joshua 1:9 (NIV).

2. Gideon: Called While Afraid

When God called Gideon, he was hiding. Yet God called him **"mighty warrior"** (see **Judges 6:12**), not because of how he felt, but because of who he was in God's eyes. Gideon eventually overcame fear and led Israel to victory.

3. Peter: Stepping Out on the Water

Peter walked on water—until he let fear distract him. But even then, when he began to sink, Jesus reached for him. Fear may cause you to stumble, but grace will still catch you if your heart is pointed toward Jesus.

Fear Distorts the View

Fear exaggerates risk and minimizes reward. It says:

- "The giants are too big" (see Numbers 13:33).
- "I'm not qualified."
- "There's too much opposition."

But God says:

- "You are well able" (see Numbers 13:30).
- "My grace is sufficient" (see 2 Corinthians 12:9).
- "No weapon formed against you shall prosper" (see Isaiah 54:17).

You Don't Have to Be Perfect—Just Willing

Fear often disguises itself as caution or wisdom, but if it's keeping you from obeying God, it's not from Him. God never asks for perfect courage—He asks for trust.

You don't need to have it all together. You just have to say, *"Yes, Lord,"* and take one step forward. With every step, fear loses power, and faith gains ground.

Key Scriptures

- 2 Timothy 1:7
- Joshua 1:9
- 1 John 4:18
- Isaiah 41:10
- Psalm 27:1

Reflection Questions

1. What fear has been standing at the threshold of your next step?

2. Are you listening more to the voice of fear or the voice of God?

3. What would you do today if fear weren't a factor?

Declaration

Fear has no power over me. I have not been given a spirit of fear, but of power, love, and a sound mind. I will walk through every open door, not because I am fearless, but because I trust the One who opens the door. I refuse to let fear make my decisions.

Prayer

Father, I surrender every fear—fear of failure, fear of rejection, fear of the unknown. I know You did not give me a spirit of fear, but of boldness and strength. I choose to move forward in faith. Help me to trust You more than I trust my fears. Thank You for the open door and the grace to walk through it. In Jesus' name. Amen.

Chapter 6

Overcoming Obstacles at the Threshold

"because a great door for effective work has opened to me, and there are many who oppose me." —1 Corinthians 16:9 (NIV)

The Door Is Open–But So Is Opposition

When God opens a door in your life, it does not mean the path will be free of resistance. In fact, sometimes the greatest confirmation that a door is from God is the presence of spiritual, emotional, or circumstantial obstacles right at the threshold.

Paul said a "great door" was open to him for effective work, but there were many adversaries. That's the paradox of purpose: every divine opportunity comes with demonic opposition.

The Threshold Is the Testing Ground

The threshold—the place between where you've been and where God is taking you—is often where the biggest battles take place:

- Doubt questions your ability.
- Distractions arise to pull you off course.
- Delays tempt you to turn back.
- Discouragement makes you question your direction.

But hear this: just because you're encountering resistance doesn't mean you're going the wrong way. It often means you're going the right way—and the enemy knows it.

Opposition Cannot Close What God Has Opened

"What he opens no one can shut, and what he shuts no one can open." —Revelation 3:7 (NIV)

Obstacles may delay your progress, but they cannot override God's sovereignty. What God has set before you is secure. The only way to miss it is to stop walking in faith.

Example: The Walls of Jericho

In Joshua 6, the Israelites stood before Jericho—a city that represented the first barrier to possessing the Promised Land. The door to Canaan was open, but Jericho was the obstacle.

God gave them instructions: march, be silent, obey, and shout when the time is right. Their obedience brought a supernatural breakthrough.

Likewise, the obstacle you face is not meant to stop you; it's meant to reveal God's power through your obedience.

Common Obstacles at the Threshold

- **People** – Naysayers, critics, or even loved ones who doubt your calling.
- **Past mistakes** – Guilt and shame can keep you from moving forward.

- **Impatience** – Wanting instant results instead of trusting the process.
- **Distraction** – Getting busy with things that aren't part of your assignment.
- **Fatigue** – Physical, emotional, or spiritual exhaustion.

"And let us not be weary in well doing: for in due season we shall reap, if we faint not." —Galatians 6:9 (KJV)

How to Overcome the Obstacles

1. Anchor in the Word

When Jesus was tempted in the wilderness, He used the Word to fight. So must we.

"It is written…" —Matthew 4:4 (KJV).

2. Speak to the Mountain

Jesus taught His disciples to speak to obstacles, not accept them.

"If you have faith as small as a mustard seed… you can say to this mountain, 'Move…' and it will move." —Matthew 17:20 (NIV).

3. Stay in Prayer and Worship

These are spiritual weapons. They disarm fear and release divine strategies.

"For the weapons of our warfare are not carnal, but mighty through God…" —2 Corinthians 10:4 (KJV).

4. Stay Focused

Don't look back. Don't look down. Keep your eyes on Jesus and the goal ahead.

"Let your eyes look straight ahead; fix your gaze directly before you." —Proverbs 4:25 (NIV).

Key Scriptures

- 1 Corinthians 16:9
- Galatians 6:9
- Joshua 6:1–20
- 2 Corinthians 10:4
- Matthew 17:20
- Proverbs 4:25

Reflection Questions

1. What obstacles are currently standing between you and your next step?

2. Have you mistaken resistance as a sign that the door is closed?

3. How can you activate your faith today to overcome what's blocking your progress?

Declaration

I will not be moved by obstacles. What God has opened for me, no man, no attack, and no fear can shut. I declare that resistance will not stop my obedience. I am advancing by faith through every open door set before me.

Prayer

Father, thank You that no opposition can cancel Your purpose for my life. Give me strength to press through every obstacle with faith and perseverance. Teach me to speak truth in the face of resistance, and help me to keep my eyes fixed on You. I trust that You will bring me through the threshold into all You've prepared. In Jesus' name. Amen.

Chapter 7

Preparation for What's Beyond the Door

"If you have run with the footmen, and they have wearied you, then how can you contend with horses?" —Jeremiah 12:5 (NKJV)

More Than a Moment—It's a Mission

Every open door leads to something greater. It's not just an opportunity; it's an assignment. And before God allows you to fully step into what's beyond the threshold, He prepares you.

The open door is not the finish line—it's the beginning of a new level of responsibility, influence, and purpose. That's why preparation is essential. If you walk through without the right posture, the right heart, and the right tools, the very opportunity meant to bless you can overwhelm you.

God Prepares the Person Before He Unfolds the Purpose

Consider this: before David ever sat on the throne, he served in the pasture. Before Esther stood before the king, she submitted to a year of preparation. Before Jesus began His public ministry, He spent 40 days in the wilderness and 30 years in obscurity.

Pastor Dr. Claudine Benjamin

God prepares in secret what He intends to use in public.

"Humble yourselves therefore under God's mighty hand, that he may lift you up in due time." —1 Peter 5:6 (KJV)

Preparation protects you. It builds the endurance, character, and spiritual maturity required for what is to come.

The Danger of Rushing Through the Door

When you skip preparation, the weight of what's beyond the door can crush you:

- Promotion without process leads to pride.
- Influence without discipline leads to burnout.
- Visibility without maturity leads to compromise.

God opens doors not just because you're ready to be seen, but because you're ready to serve. That readiness is forged in private moments of prayer, study, fasting, and obedience.

Example: Joseph's Journey

Joseph received a dream as a teenager, but it took over 13 years of betrayal, prison, and perseverance before he stepped through the open door of leadership in Egypt (see Genesis 37–41). His preparation built the integrity needed to preserve a nation.

"Until the time came to fulfill his dreams, the Lord tested Joseph's character." —Psalm 105:19 (NLT)

What Does Preparation Look Like?

- **Spiritual Maturity** – Growing in your walk with God through prayer, fasting, worship, and the Word.

- **Character Development** – Letting God refine areas of pride, impatience, or insecurity.

- **Discipleship and Mentorship** – Submitting to wise counsel and accountability.

- **Stewardship** – Managing your current responsibilities with excellence.

- **Humility** – Staying teachable and faithful in the small things.

"Whoever can be trusted with very little can also be trusted with much..." —Luke 16:10 (NIV)

Questions to Ask in the Season of Preparation

- Am I developing the fruit of the Spirit or only focusing on gifts and talents?
- Have I submitted my desires to God's timing?
- Is my character strong enough to carry the weight of greater influence?
- What spiritual disciplines am I building into my daily life?

You Are in Training, Not in Trouble

Sometimes, we mistake preparation seasons as punishment. But they are actually signs of divine trust. God invests in those He intends to use.

Don't despise the season of development. It's not delaying you; it's equipping you. What you learn in the quiet will sustain you in the spotlight.

"But they that wait upon the Lord shall renew their strength…"
—Isaiah 40:31 (KJV).

Key Scriptures

- Jeremiah 12:5
- 1 Peter 5:6
- Psalm 105:19
- Luke 16:10
- Isaiah 40:31

Reflection Questions

1. Are you embracing the season of preparation or resisting it?

2. What specific areas is God asking you to grow in before you enter what's next?

3. How can you better steward your "now" while waiting for your "next"?

Declaration

Lord, I welcome the season of preparation. I will not rush the process. I trust that You are refining, equipping, and maturing me for what lies beyond the open door. I declare that I will be ready in character, faith, and humility to carry what You entrust to me.

Prayer

Father, thank You for loving me enough to prepare me for what's ahead. Help me to embrace the process, grow in grace, and walk in obedience every step of the way. I surrender my timeline to You and ask for the patience and discipline to be made ready. In Jesus' name. Amen.

Chapter 8

When God Shuts Other Doors

"Trust in the Lord with all your heart, and lean not on your own understanding; in all your ways acknowledge Him, and He shall direct your paths." —Proverbs 3:5–6 (NKJV)

A Closed Door Is Not a Rejection—It's a Redirection

We often rejoice when doors open, but we wrestle when doors close. Yet the same God who opens doors is also the One who closes them. And both actions are equally acts of His grace.

Just because a door closes doesn't mean God is punishing you. Sometimes, He's protecting you. Other times, He's positioning you for a greater opportunity. Closed doors are not the end—they are divine detours that realign us with God's perfect will.

"What He opens no one can shut, and what He shuts no one can open." —Revelation 3:7 (NIV)

When God closes a door, no amount of effort, manipulation, or striving can pry it back open. He does it out of mercy, because He sees what we cannot.

Learning to Trust God's "No"

- Trusting God when He says "yes" is easy. Trusting Him when He says "no" is where faith matures.
- You may not have gotten that job because the environment would have poisoned your purpose.
- That relationship may have ended because it would've led to distraction, not destiny.
- That ministry door may have closed because God is preserving you for a different assignment.

"The Lord is my shepherd; I shall not want. He makes me to lie down in green pastures; He leads me beside the still waters." — Psalm 23:1–2 (NKJV).

Sometimes the Shepherd closes a gate because there's a wolf waiting on the other side.

Biblical Examples of Closed Doors

1. Paul in Asia

Paul, the apostle of the open door, experienced a closed one:

"Now when they had gone throughout Phrygia and the region of Galatia, and were forbidden of the Holy Ghost to preach the word in Asia." —Acts 16:6 (KJV).

God closed the door—not because Paul was in sin, but because He had a better door in Macedonia. Paul's redirection led to the salvation of Lydia and the Philippian jailer—eternal fruit from a divine detour.

2. Jesus at Nazareth

Even Jesus had doors closed in His own hometown.

"And he did not do many miracles there because of their lack of faith." —Matthew 13:58 (NIV)

Rejection in one place didn't hinder His mission—it redirected Him to where hearts were ready.

3. Noah and the Ark

When the flood began, it was not Noah who closed the door to the ark—it was God (see Genesis 7:16). God sealed that door as an act of protection and judgment.

Some doors are closed to save you, not to stop you.

Signs That God Is Closing a Door

- No peace despite persistent effort.
- Consistent barriers without progress.
- Divine delays that expose your impatience.
- Spiritual conviction or caution.
- Wise counsel pointing in another direction.

What to Do When the Door Closes

- **Don't Panic—Pray**

Ask God for clarity, not just relief.

- **Wait with Expectation**

A closed door today may open to a new assignment tomorrow.

- **Redirect Your Focus**

Ask: *"Lord, what are You trying to teach me or protect me from?"*

- **Keep Moving in Faith**

A "no" here is often a "yes" somewhere else.

"In their hearts humans plan their course, but the Lord establishes their steps." —Proverbs 16:9 (NIV).

Key Scriptures

- Proverbs 3:5–6
- Revelation 3:7
- Acts 16:6–10
- Matthew 13:58
- Genesis 7:16
- Isaiah 55:8–9

Reflection Questions

1. Have you been resisting a closed door that God is using to redirect you?

2. What have you learned in your waiting or redirection season?

3. Are you willing to surrender your will to God's timing and path?

Declaration

I trust God, even when I don't understand the 'why.' I believe that every closed door is His way of protecting, guiding, and preparing me for something greater. I release my frustration and embrace His redirection with faith and peace.

Prayer

Father, thank You for every door You've opened—and for every door You've closed. Help me to trust You when the path changes, and to believe that Your "no" is still filled with love. Strengthen my heart in the waiting, and sharpen my discernment for the next step. I know that Your plan is perfect, and I choose to follow You. In Jesus' name. Amen.

Chapter 9

Doors of Ministry, Opportunity, and Promotion

"A man's gift makes room for him, and brings him before great men." —Proverbs 18:16 (NKJV)

Every Open Door Has a Divine Purpose

When God opens a door, it's never random. His openings are intentional—strategically timed for ministry, opportunity, and promotion. These doors are not simply for personal gain or applause. They are for kingdom advancement, divine influence, and supernatural fulfillment of calling.

Whether you're called to preach, lead, teach, build, serve, or create—God uses open doors to position His people in places of impact. But you must recognize that every open door comes with responsibility.

"...to whom men have committed much, of him they will ask the more." —Luke 12:48 (KJV).

Ministry Doors: Called to Serve

God opens doors of ministry not just to elevate us, but to equip and bless others. True ministry isn't about platforms—it's about people. Every open door to preach, teach, lead, or serve is an opportunity to reflect Jesus.

Paul's Testimony

"Pray also for us, that God may open to us a door for the word, to declare the mystery of Christ..." —Colossians 4:3 (ESV)

Paul didn't pray for ease—he prayed for opportunity. Ministry doors require courage, faithfulness, and a willingness to be used, even in uncomfortable places.

Opportunity Doors: Positioned for Purpose

There are moments in life when God opens doors in careers, education, finances, or relationships—not just for your benefit, but so you can be a vessel for His glory.

Example: Esther

Esther walked through a door into the palace, but not for luxury. God positioned her **"for such a time as this"** (see **Esther 4:14**) to save a nation. Her opportunity was her assignment. Likewise, your promotion is not the goal—it's the gateway to influence.

"But I have raised you up for this very purpose, that I might show you my power and that my name might be proclaimed in all the earth." —Exodus 9:16 (NIV)

Promotion Doors: Lifted for Kingdom Impact

Promotion is not just about going higher—it's about being trusted with more. True promotion in God's kingdom is always connected to stewardship, character, and assignment.

"Humble yourselves, therefore, under God's mighty hand, that he may lift you up in due time." —1 Peter 5:6 (NIV)

God promotes those who are faithful in secret. Joseph was promoted to the palace because he was faithful in the prison. David was anointed king because he was faithful with sheep.

Don't seek the door of promotion—seek the heart of God. The door will follow.

How to Steward Doors of Ministry, Opportunity, and Promotion

- **Remain Humble** – Promotion is a platform for service, not self-glory.

- **Stay Prayerful** – Every opportunity must be bathed in prayer.

- **Be Accountable** – Stay connected to wise counsel.

- **Don't Forget the Mission** – Open doors are about kingdom expansion, not personal advancement.

- **Walk in Excellence** – Represent Christ with diligence and integrity.

Warnings About Open Doors

- Not every open door is from God. In Matthew 4:8–10, Satan offered Jesus a door.
- Be discerning. Pray for confirmation, not just comfort.

- Promotion without purpose leads to pride. Ask God for alignment before acceleration.

Key Scriptures

- Proverbs 18:16
- Colossians 4:3
- Esther 4:14
- 1 Peter 5:6
- Luke 12:48
- Exodus 9:16

Reflection Questions

1. What open door are you standing in right now, and how are you stewarding it?

2. Are you seeking promotion, or are you seeking God's purpose?

3. How can your current opportunity serve someone else and glorify God?

Declaration

I thank You, Lord, for every door of ministry, opportunity, and promotion. I declare that I will walk in humility, purpose, and boldness. I will not be distracted by status or applause. I will serve with excellence and keep my eyes on You, the Door-opener and Destiny-giver.

Prayer

Father, thank You for every door You open in my life. Whether it leads to a pulpit or a palace, let my heart remain humble and my hands ready to serve. Help me to walk in purpose and use every opportunity to glorify You. Keep me aligned with Your will, and let every promotion draw me closer to Your heart. In Jesus' name, amen.

Chapter 10

Persistence Pays Off

"Let us not become weary in doing good, for at the proper time we will reap a harvest if we do not give up." —Galatians 6:9 (NIV)

Open Doors Often Require Persistent Faith

Some doors do not swing wide immediately. They may open gradually, after seasons of testing, praying, and waiting. The truth is, the right door is not only about God's timing—it's also about our persistence. God wants to know: Will you keep knocking?

Jesus emphasized this truth in Luke 18 when He told the parable of the persistent widow. She refused to give up until she got justice. Though she faced delay, she did not accept denial.

"And will not God bring about justice for His chosen ones, who cry out to Him day and night?" —Luke 18:7 (NIV)

Persistence doesn't change God—it prepares you. It shapes your character, sharpens your faith, and reveals how much you trust Him.

Don't Confuse Delay with Denial

Many believers walk away right before the door opens. The process wore them down. The wait broke their hope. But what if the moment you feel like giving up is the exact moment you're closest to a breakthrough?

"For you have need of endurance, so that after you have done the will of God, you may receive the promise." —Hebrews 10:36 (NKJV)

God often waits until we've reached the end of ourselves so that He gets the glory—not our gifts, connections, or cleverness.

Examples of Persistence in Scripture

1. Elijah's Servant and the Cloud

Elijah told his servant to look for rain after praying. The servant saw nothing—six times. But Elijah said, "Go again."

The seventh time the servant reported, "A cloud as small as a man's hand is rising from the sea." —1 Kings 18:44 (NIV)

Breakthrough showed up not on the first look, but on the seventh.

2. The Syrophoenician Woman

She was not of Jewish descent, yet she persisted in asking Jesus to heal her daughter. Despite the silence and resistance, she didn't back down.

"Woman, you have great faith! Your request is granted." — Matthew 15:28 (NIV)

Persistence turned a closed door into a miraculous moment.

3. Jacob Wrestling with God

Jacob said, **"I will not let You go unless You bless me"** (see **Genesis 32:26**). He wrestled through the night and walked away limping—but changed and blessed.

Persistence requires a grip that will not let go of God's promise, no matter what.

What Are You Persisting In?

God is calling His people to pray persistently, obey consistently, and believe relentlessly. Don't be passive in your pursuit of what God has promised.

- Are you waiting on a door of healing? Don't stop praying.
- Waiting on a door of provision? Keep declaring and trusting.
- Waiting on a door of restoration? Keep sowing love and forgiveness.

The harvest is promised, but it comes to those who do not faint.

How to Cultivate Persistence

- **Daily Prayer** – Keep your communication with God strong.

- **Scripture Meditation** – Feed your faith with truth.

- **Worship Through Waiting** – Praise, even when you don't see the outcome.

- **Accountability** – Walk with others who will encourage you not to give up.

- **Vision Reminders** – Keep God's promise in front of your eyes (see Habakkuk 2:2).

"For the revelation awaits an appointed time; it speaks of the end and will not prove false. Though it linger, wait for it; it will certainly come and will not delay." —Habakkuk 2:3

Key Scriptures

- Galatians 6:9
- Luke 18:1–8
- 1 Kings 18:44
- Genesis 32:26
- Hebrews 10:36
- Habakkuk 2:3

Reflection Questions

1. What open door have you been praying about but feel tempted to quit pursuing?

2. Are you pressing forward in faith—or backing off in frustration?

3. What disciplines can you renew today to keep going?

Declaration

I will not grow weary in doing good. I believe that the harvest is coming. Even when I don't see the full result, I trust God's timing. I declare that my persistence in prayer, faith, and obedience will produce fruit. I will not give up!

Prayer

Lord, strengthen my heart to persist in the face of delay. I choose to trust You beyond what I see. Help me to be steadfast, immovable, always abounding in the work You've called me to. Let me never let go of the promises You've spoken over my life. I believe that what You've spoken will come to pass. In Jesus' name. Amen.

Chapter 11

Discerning Counterfeit Doors

"See, I have placed before you an open door that no one can shut." —Revelation 3:8 (NIV)

Every open door is not a God door.

In a world full of distractions, fast options, and shiny opportunities, it can be dangerously easy to walk through a door that looks like favor—but is really a counterfeit. As believers, we must learn to discern what God has truly opened versus what the enemy has crafted as a distraction, delay, or even destruction.

The enemy doesn't always come as a roaring lion. Sometimes he comes as a seemingly perfect opportunity.

This chapter is a call to spiritual maturity, urging us to test, pray, and wait when necessary. Just because something is available doesn't mean it's appointed. And just because it's easy doesn't mean it's ordained.

The Nature of the Open Door

When God opens a door, it carries His fingerprints:

- It aligns with His Word.
- It brings peace, not confusion.
- It draws you closer to Him, not further away.

- It requires faith, but not compromise.

Revelation 3:8 says, **"See, I have placed before you an open door that no one can shut."** Notice—God places it. Not man. Not manipulation. Not ambition. It is sovereign. It is specific. And it cannot be revoked.

God's doors are often preceded by prayer, preparation, and peace. Counterfeit doors are often rushed, forced, and cloaked in temptation.

The Danger of the Counterfeit

Satan is a deceiver. If he can't destroy you with outright sin, he'll try to distract you with a detour.

2 Corinthians 11:14 says, **"Satan himself masquerades as an angel of light." (NIV).** That means the enemy knows how to disguise a trap as a blessing. He might send:

- A relationship that looks godly but pulls you from your calling.
- A job that pays more but compromises your integrity.
- A platform that feeds your ego but starves your soul.

Discernment is not suspicion. It is Spirit-led awareness. It is the ability to pause and ask: Is this from God, or does it just look good?

Eve didn't fall for something ugly—she fell for something **"desirable for gaining wisdom" (see Genesis 3:6).**

How to Test the Door

- **Test it by the Word of God.**

God will never open a door that contradicts His Word. If the opportunity requires you to lie, manipulate, compromise, or walk in pride, it is not from Him.

- **Test it by peace.**

Colossians 3:15 says, **"Let the peace of Christ rule in your hearts..." (NIV).** If your spirit feels unsettled, agitated, or divided, pause. God's peace is a divine compass.

- **Test it in prayer.**

Ask the Holy Spirit: *"Is this Your will for me?"* God doesn't play hide and seek. James 1:5 promises wisdom to those who ask.

- **Test it with timing.**

Some doors are right, but the timing is wrong. If you're being pressured to rush, it may not be God. The enemy pushes. God leads.

- **Test it with counsel.**

Proverbs 11:14 says, **"In the multitude of counselors there is safety." (KJV).** Wise mentors and spiritual leaders can help confirm what you're hearing.

When God Closes a Door

Sometimes we mourn closed doors that were actually God's mercy. We cry over rejection, not realizing it was divine protection. God sees what we can't see—and a closed door is often a setup for a better one.

If God closed it, trust Him. Don't kick open what He's locked. Don't beg for what He blocked. If you walk through a door He didn't open, you'll be responsible for sustaining what He never ordained.

Stay Close to the Doorkeeper

In **John 10:9**, Jesus says, **"I am the door." (KJV).**

This is the most powerful truth of all: Jesus is not just the One who opens doors—He is the Door.

That means our focus shouldn't be on chasing opportunities, but on staying close to Him. The closer you are to the Door, the more clearly you can see what's real and what's counterfeit.

When you abide in the presence of God, counterfeit doors lose their appeal. When you're filled with the Spirit, you recognize when something's off, even if it looks good on the surface.

Key Scriptures

- Revelation 3:8
- 2 Corinthians 11:14
- Genesis 3:6
- James 1:5

- Colossians 3:15
- John 10:9
- Proverbs 11:14

Reflection Questions

1. Have you ever walked through a door that you later realized was not from God?

2. What doors in your life right now need prayerful testing?

3. Are you willing to wait for God's best instead of rushing into what looks convenient?

Declaration

I declare that I walk in discernment. I will not be deceived by counterfeit doors. The Spirit of God leads me into truth. I wait for divine timing. I trust the Doorkeeper, and I follow His voice. I will not rush, settle, or compromise. The door God opens for me, no one can shut—and I will walk through it in confidence and peace.

Prayer

Lord Jesus, You are the Door. You are my Shepherd and my Guide. In a world full of noise, choices, and distractions, help me to see clearly. Sharpen my discernment so I do not confuse opportunity with obedience. Teach me to test every open door by Your Word, Your peace, Your timing, and Your Spirit. When You close a door, help me trust that it was for my protection. When You open one, give me the courage to walk through it with faith. I surrender my ambition, impatience, and desire for quick fixes. Keep me close to

You, the Doorkeeper, so that I may know what is truly from You. Let no counterfeit distract me from Your best. In Your name, Jesus, I pray. Amen.

Chapter 12

Waiting for the Right Timing

"To every thing there is a season, and a time to every purpose under the heaven:" —Ecclesiastes 3:1 (KJV)

God can open a door for you, but He still asks you to wait before walking through it.

This is one of the hardest truths to embrace in our spiritual journey. We see the opportunity, we feel the calling, we sense the shift—but God whispers, *"Not yet."* Waiting doesn't mean denial. It means preparation. And timing is everything in the kingdom of God.

In **Revelation 3:8**, Jesus says, **"I have set before you an open door..."** But even divine doors must be walked through with divine timing.

The Tension of Timing

Often, we confuse the presence of an open door with permission to proceed. But doors can open before you're ready. And what you enter prematurely can become a burden instead of a blessing.

There is a holy tension between promise and fulfillment. Think of David. Anointed as king while still a teenager, but he didn't step onto the throne until years later. The door was open, the oil had been poured—but the timing wasn't right.

The same happened with Joseph. He had a dream of promotion, but he was betrayed, enslaved, and imprisoned before ever standing in Pharaoh's court. The dream was divine, but the process was essential.

Why the Wait?

Here's why God sometimes delays your entrance, even to doors He Himself opened:

- **Preparation of character**

What God is calling you to requires maturity. He loves you too much to give you something that will crush you.

- **Alignment of circumstances**

God often arranges situations, relationships, and environments before releasing you into a new space.

- **Protection from premature warfare**

Some doors lead into battlegrounds. If you're not spiritually ready, you'll face attacks you weren't equipped to endure.

- **Teaching you to trust the Giver, not the gift**

Waiting refines your worship. It shifts your focus from the door to the Doorkeeper—and that is exactly where your security should lie.

The Danger of Moving Too Soon

In 1 Samuel 13, King Saul grew impatient while waiting for Samuel to offer the sacrifice. Because he didn't wait, he stepped out of alignment with God's instruction—and it cost him his kingdom.

Impatience can rob you of your inheritance. The right door at the wrong time is still a wrong move.

Isaiah 28:16 says, **"Whoever believes will not act hastily."** **(NKJV).** Rushed decisions are often a sign of fear, not faith. If God said He opened the door, He will also tell you when to walk through it.

You don't need to force it. You don't need to beg. And you definitely don't need to compete. What is truly yours is never at risk when you wait on God.

What to Do While You Wait

Waiting isn't passive. It's an active season of preparation and obedience. Here's how you can wait well:

- **Worship in the waiting.** Praise aligns your heart with God's presence and keeps you focused on Him, not the outcome.

- **Pray for clarity.** Ask God to continue revealing what's for you and what's not.

- **Sharpen your skills.** Use this time to grow, learn, serve, and build.

- **Walk in obedience.** Sometimes the next door opens when you've fully obeyed in the current room.

Psalm 27:14 encourages us: **"Wait on the Lord; be of good courage, and He shall strengthen your heart; wait, I say, on the Lord!" (NKJV).** Waiting takes strength. But the wait is always worth it.

God's Timing Is Perfect

You may feel delayed, but you are not denied.

You may feel ready, but God sees deeper. He knows the right season, the right place, the right timing, and the right pace for your entrance.

Habakkuk 2:3 says, **"For the vision is yet for an appointed time; but at the end it will speak, and it will not lie. Though it tarries, wait for it; because it will surely come, it will not tarry."** That means once God's appointed time hits your life, nothing can stop it. But if you walk ahead of Him, you may enter a door you're not graced to stand in.

Waiting is not a punishment—it's a strategy.

Key Scriptures

- Ecclesiastes 3:1
- Revelation 3:8

- Psalm 27:14
- Habakkuk 2:3
- Isaiah 28:16
- 1 Samuel 13:8–14

Reflection Questions

1. Are there any open doors in your life that you're tempted to rush through?

2. How has God used past waiting seasons to strengthen you?

3. What can you do right now to prepare for what's next?

Declaration

I declare that I trust God's timing. I will not rush ahead, nor will I lag behind. I walk in step with the Holy Spirit. I will not act hastily, because my confidence is in the Lord. The doors He opens for me will be entered at the appointed time, and they will lead to divine purpose, peace, and power.

Prayer

Father, You are the God of perfect timing. Even when I see the door open, help me not to run ahead of You. Teach me to wait with trust, to rest without striving, and to prepare with faith. Strengthen my heart in the quiet seasons, and remind me that delay is not denial. Help me to fix my eyes on You, not the opportunity—on the Doorkeeper, not the door. I believe that what You've ordained will come to pass at the appointed time. Until then, I will worship, obey, and grow in Your presence. In Jesus' name. Amen.

Chapter 13

Boldly Stepping Forward

"Have I not commanded you? Be strong and courageous. Do not be afraid; do not be discouraged, for the Lord your God will be with you wherever you go." —Joshua 1:9 (NIV)

The Door Is Open—Now It's Time to Move

Many believers stand at the edge of a breakthrough, positioned before an open door—but never step through. The invitation is real, the timing is right, and the Spirit is stirring—yet hesitation grips the heart.

God never opens a door just for observation; He opens it for occupation. The open door is not a window for admiration—it is an entrance for movement.

"Faith without works is dead." —James 2:26 (KJV)

To walk through what God has prepared, you must act. You must step forward in faith, courage, and obedience—even when you feel unqualified, uncertain, or underprepared.

Courage Is a Command, Not a Suggestion

When God told Joshua to lead Israel into the Promised Land, He didn't ask him to be courageous—He commanded it.

"Only be thou strong and very courageous, that thou mayest observe to do according to all the law, which Moses my servant commanded thee: turn not from it to the right hand or to the left, that thou mayest prosper withersoever thou goest." — Joshua 1:7 (KJV)

Joshua's courage wasn't rooted in his experience—it was rooted in God's presence. The same God who opened the Jordan was the God who would lead them through Jericho.

You may not have all the answers. But if you have God's assurance, that's enough.

Boldness Honors God

Boldness is not arrogance—it is confidence in God's faithfulness. When you step out in faith, you're declaring:

- "God's Word is true."
- "God's grace is enough."
- "God's presence goes before me."

"Seeing then that we have such hope, we use great plainness of speech:" —2 Corinthians 3:12 (KJV)

Bold faith brings glory to God because it relies fully on Him. Heaven celebrates the moment you say, *"I'm going through this door no matter what it costs me."*

The Risk of Staying Still

Staying safe can be more dangerous than stepping out. Comfort zones often become stagnation zones. When we refuse to move forward, we risk:

- Delaying destiny.
- Missing moments.
- Settling for less than God's best.

"Now the just shall live by faith: but if any man draw back, my soul shall have no pleasure in him." —Hebrews 10:38 (KJV)

The cost of passivity is too high. Your future demands movement.

Steps to Boldly Move Forward

1. Rehearse God's Promises

Let His Word silence your fear.

"Your word is a lamp to my feet and a light to my path." — Psalm 119:105 (NKJV)

2. Silence Doubt

Refuse to let inner insecurity talk you out of obedience.

3. Take the First Step

God often reveals the next level after you take the first action.

4. Surround Yourself with Faith-Filled Voices

Joshua and Caleb moved forward. The other ten spies fed fear. Choose your company wisely.

5. Keep Your Eyes on the One Who Called You

Peter walked on water—until he looked at the waves (see Matthew 14:30). Keep your focus on Christ, not the chaos.

Key Scriptures

- Joshua 1:9
- James 2:26
- 2 Corinthians 3:12
- Hebrews 10:38
- Psalm 119:105
- Matthew 14:30

Reflection Questions

1. What door are you standing in front of but afraid to step through?

2. What bold move is God asking you to take this week?

3. Are you waiting for everything to be perfect, or are you willing to move with faith?

Declaration

I will not be paralyzed by fear or uncertainty. I am bold because the Lord my God is with me. I will take action in faith, trusting that the

God who opened the door will sustain me on the path. I move forward with courage, not in my strength, but in His.

Prayer

Lord, thank You for the open door before me. Fill me with holy courage to step forward, even when I don't see the full picture. I trust You. I surrender fear and choose obedience. Let my movement honor You, and let every step bring me closer to the fullness of my assignment. In Jesus' name. Amen.

Chapter 14

Staying Humble After the Door Opens

**"Humble yourselves before the Lord, and He will lift you up."
—James 4:10 (NIV)**

The Greatest Test of Character Is Not the Wait—It's the Success

Many people pray for open doors, fast for favor, and labor in obscurity until God brings them into new levels of influence, ministry, or blessing. But once they step into that open door, a subtle and dangerous temptation arises: pride.

The greatest threat after promotion is forgetting the One who opened the door in the first place.

**"When you have eaten and are satisfied, praise the Lord your God... Be careful that you do not forget the Lord your God."
—Deuteronomy 8:10–11 (NIV)**

God promotes the humble, but He resists the proud. Staying low while going high is the posture of a kingdom-minded believer.

Promotion Is a Platform for Service, Not Superiority

When God lifts you, it's never for status—it's for service. The higher the position, the greater the responsibility. Humility keeps your heart aligned with God's heart.

"...the Son of Man did not come to be served, but to serve..."
—Matthew 20:28 (NIV)

Even Jesus, the door Himself (see **John 10:9**), walked through the door of divine purpose with humility, servanthood, and obedience unto death. He is our model.

Example: King Saul vs. King David

- Saul was elevated quickly but fell due to pride and disobedience.
- David, though flawed, remained a man after God's heart because he knew who made him king and repented when wrong.

"He chose David his servant and took him from the sheep pens; from tending the sheep he brought him to be the shepherd of his people Jacob, of Israel his inheritance. And David shepherded them with integrity of heart; with skillful hands he led them." —Psalm 78:70–72 (NIV)

Signs That Pride Is Creeping In

- You stop seeking God's counsel.
- You crave credit more than fruit.
- You avoid accountability.
- You compare or compete instead of serve.
- You begin to believe your elevation is proof of superiority.

Pride blinds you to the truth. Humility keeps you teachable, grateful, and grounded.

How to Remain Humble After Promotion

1. Remember Who Opened the Door

"Every good and perfect gift is from above..." —James 1:17 (NIV)

2. Give God the Glory Publicly

Don't let people celebrate your strength without hearing about your Source.

3. Stay Rooted in the Word and Prayer

Promotion should deepen your devotion, not distract from it.

4. Serve Others Consistently

Jesus washed feet. You are never too promoted to serve.

5. Remain Accountable

Submit to wise counsel, mentors, and spiritual leaders who speak the truth in love.

"Pride goes before destruction, a haughty spirit before a fall." —Proverbs 16:18 (NIV)

Key Scriptures

- James 4:10

- Deuteronomy 8:10–11
- Matthew 20:28
- John 10:9
- Proverbs 16:18
- James 1:17
- Psalm 78:70–72

Reflection Questions

1. Has success made you more dependent on God, or less?

2. Are you still serving with the same passion as before the door opened?

3. Who in your life keeps you grounded and accountable?

Declaration

I will walk through every open door with humility and gratitude. I will never forget the God who opened it for me. I declare that promotion will not change my posture—I will stay low, serve well, and give God all the glory. I choose to live lifted, yet humble.

Prayer

Lord, I thank You for every opportunity You've given me. I acknowledge that every open door is a result of Your grace, not my strength. Keep my heart humble. Let success never distract me from You. Teach me to serve faithfully, lead with integrity, and give You all the glory. In Jesus' name. Amen.

Chapter 15

Faithfulness to the Assignment

"Now it is required that those who have been given a trust must prove faithful." —1 Corinthians 4:2 (NIV)

The Door Was Never the Goal—The Assignment Is

When God sets before you an open door, it's not an endpoint—it's a beginning. Every door leads to a responsibility, a mission, a divine assignment. Walking through the door is only step one. What matters next is your faithfulness to what God has entrusted you with on the other side.

"Who then is the faithful and wise servant, whom the master has put in charge…?" —Matthew 24:45 (NIV)

God honors the faithful, not just the gifted. He measures obedience over outcome and commitment over charisma.

Success is Measured in Faithfulness, Not Fame

In a culture obsessed with results, God looks for something deeper: endurance and consistency. You may not always feel fruitful, but you can remain faithful. And in God's kingdom, that's what counts.

Example: Noah

Noah was faithful in an assignment that made no sense in the natural. He built the ark over decades with no evidence of rain. His obedience saved generations.

"Noah did everything just as God commanded him." —Genesis 6:22 (NIV)

He wasn't famous—he was faithful. And that's what secured his place in God's purpose.

Staying Focused on Your God-Given Assignment

Open doors often bring more responsibilities, more visibility, and more spiritual pressure. It becomes easy to drift into comparison, competition, or compromise. But God calls you to remain anchored to the assignment, not the applause.

Stay committed to:

- The vision God gave you.
- The people He's called you to serve.
- The boundaries that guard your integrity.
- The pace that aligns with His will, not the rush of others.

"Therefore, since we are surrounded by such a great cloud of witnesses, let us throw off everything that hinders and the sin that so easily entangles. And let us run with perseverance the race marked out for us." —Hebrews 12:1 (NIV)

The Danger of Abandoning the Assignment

- Fatigue can tempt you to quit.
- Disappointment can cause you to doubt your impact.
- Temptation can lure you into shortcuts.

But remember: the reward isn't just at the end of the door—it's at the end of the assignment.

"Well done, good and faithful servant." —Matthew 25:21 (NIV)

He doesn't say, *"Well done, talented"* or *"Well done, famous."* He says, *"Faithful."*

Ways to Remain Faithful

1. Guard Your Daily Habits

Faithfulness is built in the mundane: prayer, reading, serving, loving.

2. Refuse to Compare

Focus on your race, not someone else's door or pace.

3. Submit to God's Timing

Faithfulness is not about being fast—it's about being steady.

4. Remember Why You Started

Revisit your original calling and passion. Let it fuel you again.

5. Celebrate Small Wins

Every act of obedience matters—even when it goes unseen.

"Do not despise these small beginnings." —Zechariah 4:10 (NLT)

Key Scriptures

- 1 Corinthians 4:2
- Matthew 25:21
- Genesis 6:22
- Hebrews 12:1
- Matthew 24:45
- Zechariah 4:10

Reflection Questions

- Are you still passionate and committed to the assignment God gave you?

- Have you been measuring success by faithfulness or external results?

- What area of your life requires a fresh commitment to consistency?

Declaration

I am faithful to the assignment God has given me. I will not be swayed by pressure, applause, or opposition. I will steward every opportunity with diligence, integrity, and consistency. I declare that obedience is my success, and faithfulness is my victory.

Prayer

Lord, thank You for trusting me with this assignment. Help me to walk worthy of Your calling and remain faithful in every season. Teach me to value obedience more than recognition. Let my heart burn with renewed commitment, and may I bring You glory through steady, faithful service. In Jesus' name. Amen.

Chapter 16

Doors Opened by Prayer

"Continue earnestly in prayer, being vigilant in it with thanksgiving; meanwhile praying also for us, that God would open to us a door for the word..." —Colossians 4:2–3 (NKJV)

Prayer Precedes Every Divine Opening

Every door that God opens in the natural is first unlocked in the spiritual realm through prayer. Before opportunity appears in front of you, it is often activated by what happens behind closed doors with God.

Prayer is not just a request—it's a weapon. It aligns your heart with heaven's plan, and it moves things that human effort never could.

"The effectual fervent prayer of a righteous man availeth much." —James 5:16 (KJV)

If you're waiting for a door to open, don't just knock with effort—knock with prayer.

Paul's Example: Praying for Open Doors

In Colossians 4, the Apostle Paul specifically asked for prayer so that God would open a door for the Word. He didn't rely on reputation or strategy—he relied on prayer to prepare the way.

"And pray for us, too, that God may open a door for our message, so that we may proclaim the mystery of Christ, for which I am in chains." —Colossians 4:3 (NIV)

This teaches us: Prayer opens doors for influence, evangelism, clarity, and favor. If Paul needed prayer to move forward, how much more do we?

Prayer Changes the Atmosphere Around the Door

Sometimes doors remain shut, not because they aren't God's will, but because the spiritual atmosphere hasn't shifted yet. Persistent prayer breaks resistance in the heavenly realm.

Example: Daniel's 21-Day Prayer

Daniel fasted and prayed for 21 days before receiving his answer. The angel explained that from the first day he prayed, the answer was released—but there was warfare in the heavens (see Daniel 10:12–13). Prayer pushed through the resistance.

Then he continued, "Do not be afraid, Daniel. Since the first day that you set your mind to gain understanding and to humble yourself before your God, your words were heard, and I have come in response to them." —Daniel 10:12 (NIV)

Don't stop praying just because the door hasn't opened yet. Keep pressing—God is moving behind the scenes.

Prayer Unlocks Multiple Doors

Prayer doesn't just open one door—it can release a chain reaction of divine opportunities:

- Doors of revelation (see Jeremiah 33:3).
- Doors of wisdom and guidance (see James 1:5).
- Doors of healing and breakthrough (see Mark 11:24).
- Doors of restoration and reconciliation.
- Doors of strength when you feel too weak to move.

Every door you're waiting on is attached to your prayer life.

Types of Prayer That Open Doors

- **Intercessory Prayer** – Standing in the gap for others opens doors in their lives and yours.

- **Fasting with Prayer** – Weakens your flesh and sharpens your spiritual sensitivity.

- **Persistent Prayer** – As modeled in Luke 18, persistence wears down resistance.

- **Agreement Prayer** – Unity in prayer multiplies power (see Matthew 18:19).

- **Thanksgiving Prayer** – Gratitude in advance prepares your spirit for what's coming.

How to Pray for Open Doors

- **Be specific.** Tell God exactly what you need.
- **Pray God's Word.** Declare His promises back to Him.
- **Ask with faith.** Expect that He hears and responds.

- **Listen.** Prayer is a two-way conversation; allow space for His instructions.

"Ask and it will be given to you; seek and you will find; knock and the door will be opened to you." —Matthew 7:7 (NIV)

Key Scriptures

- Colossians 4:2–3
- James 5:16
- Daniel 10:12
- Matthew 7:7
- Luke 18:1–8
- Jeremiah 33:3

Reflection Questions

1. Have you prayed consistently about the door you are waiting on?

2. Are you trusting prayer to unlock what effort alone cannot?

3. What kind of prayer (intercession, fasting, agreement) is God calling you into for this season?

Declaration

I believe in the power of prayer. Every door God has for me will open in His perfect time, and I will partner with Him through prayer. I will not grow weary, I will not be silent—I will pray until breakthrough comes. Heaven moves when I pray.

Prayer

Father, thank You for the gift of prayer. Teach me to seek You earnestly and consistently. Let my prayers align with Your will and break every barrier standing before me. I believe You are the God who opens doors no man can shut. Let my voice be lifted in faith, and let every locked gate be opened by Your power. In Jesus' name. Amen.

Chapter 17

Maintaining Integrity at Every Stage

"The integrity of the upright guides them, but the unfaithful are destroyed by their duplicity." —Proverbs 11:3 (NIV)

Open Doors Require a Clean Heart

When God opens a door, it's not just your gifts that walk through—it's your character. The platform, promotion, or purpose beyond the door may elevate you publicly, but only integrity can keep you there.

Integrity is the invisible strength that supports your visible assignment. Without it, influence is short-lived, and open doors become missed opportunities.

"Better the poor whose walk is blameless than the rich whose ways are perverse." —Proverbs 28:6 (NIV)

The open door is never just about where you're going—it's about who you are becoming.

Integrity Is Who You Are When No One Is Watching

Integrity isn't about perfection—it's about consistency. It's the alignment of your words, your actions, and your convictions. It means:

- Telling the truth when lying would be easier.
- Honoring commitments when backing out is more comfortable.
- Resisting temptation even when no one would know.

"Whoever walks in integrity walks securely, but whoever takes crooked paths will be found out." —Proverbs 10:9 (NIV)

In a world of shortcuts, compromise, and performance, God is looking for people He can trust.

Example: Joseph

Joseph was given an open door into Pharaoh's palace, but long before that, he proved his integrity in Potiphar's house and in prison. When tempted by Potiphar's wife, he responded: **"How then could I do such a wicked thing and sin against God?" — Genesis 39:9 (NIV)**

Joseph's integrity in secret was the foundation for his influence in public.

Every Stage Requires Integrity

- **Before the Door** – Integrity in waiting seasons keeps your heart pure and your motives aligned.

- **At the Door** – Integrity gives you confidence to walk through without guilt or fear.

- **Beyond the Door** – Integrity sustains the blessing, protects your name, and honors God.

"A good name is more desirable than great riches…" — **Proverbs 22:1 (NIV)**

Temptations to Compromise

- **Pressure to Perform** – Striving to impress can lead to unethical shortcuts.

- **Pride After Promotion** – Believing you're above accountability is dangerous.

- **Private Battles** – Secret sin can silently erode your spiritual authority.

- **Cultural Norms** – The world normalizes compromise, but God's standard never changes.

Integrity is not negotiable. It must be guarded daily, tested often, and renewed through surrender.

How to Maintain Integrity Through Every Season

1. **Stay Rooted in the Word**

God's truth is your moral compass.

2. **Be Accountable**

Invite trusted leaders or friends to speak truth into your life.

3. Pray for a Clean Heart

"Create in me a pure heart, O God, and renew a steadfast spirit within me." —Psalm 51:10 (NIV)

4. Practice Honesty in the Small Things

If you're faithful in little, you'll be faithful in much (see Luke 16:10).

5. Let the Fear of God Guide You

True integrity flows from reverence for God, not fear of exposure.

Key Scriptures

- Proverbs 11:3
- Genesis 39:9
- Proverbs 10:9
- Psalm 51:10
- Proverbs 22:1
- Luke 16:10

Reflection Questions

1. Are there areas in your life where your public appearance is outpacing your private integrity?

2. How do you respond to temptation when no one is watching?

3. What guardrails or accountability can you put in place to protect your character?

Declaration

I choose integrity over image. I will walk uprightly in every season—before, during, and after the open door. My character will honor God and protect the assignment He has given me. I will not compromise. I will not pretend. I will be the same in private as I am in public, by God's grace.

Prayer

Lord, search my heart and know my thoughts. Reveal any place in me that lacks integrity, and lead me in the way everlasting. I want to walk in truth, live in purity, and lead with character. Strengthen me when I am tempted, and keep me grounded in Your Word and Your ways. In Jesus' name. Amen.

Chapter 18

Not Everyone Can Go With You

"The Lord had said to Abram, 'Go from your country, your people and your father's household to the land I will show you.'" —Genesis 12:1 (NIV)

Every Open Door Demands a Separation

As you walk through the door God has opened for you, one of the most difficult truths you'll face is this: not everyone can go with you.

There are seasons when God calls you to leave behind people, places, and patterns that no longer align with His purpose for your next level. This isn't rejection—it's refinement. God isn't trying to isolate you; He's trying to position you.

"Do two walk together unless they have agreed to do so?" — Amos 3:3 (NIV)

Sometimes the open door requires you to walk alone before you lead with others.

The Call of Abraham: A Clean Break

God told Abraham to leave behind his homeland, his family, and his comfort zone to go to a land that He would show him. This wasn't just about geography—it was about covenant. Abraham's obedience required him to break ties with his past to walk into his future.

"So Abram went, as the Lord had told him; and Lot went with him. Abram was seventy-five years old when he set out from Harran." —Genesis 12:4 (NIV)

God's instruction didn't include every detail—it included a direction. And that direction meant separation. Not everyone who was connected to Abraham was called to the same destiny.

Lot Went—But Should He Have?

Though Lot went with Abraham, his presence eventually caused strife and division. In Genesis 13, their herdsmen began to argue. Eventually, the two had to part ways.

"Is not the whole land before you? Let's part company. If you go to the left, I'll go to the right; if you go to the right, I'll go to the left." —Genesis 13:9 (NIV)

When people are attached to you but not aligned with your purpose, conflict is inevitable.

Three Types of People Who Can't Go With You

- **The Familiar** – Those who only see who you were, not who you're becoming.

- **The Comfortable** – Those who would rather stay where it's safe instead of moving forward.

- **The Draining** – Those who constantly pull you away from focus, prayer, and purpose.

- **Loyalty is important**, but loyalty to people cannot override obedience to God.

Jesus Experienced Separation Too

Even Jesus had moments where He distanced Himself:

- He sent the crowd away (see Matthew 14:22).

- He only took Peter, James, and John up the mountain (see Mark 9:2).

- He withdrew to pray alone (see Luke 5:16).

Purpose requires privacy sometimes. God will reduce your circle not to punish you, but to protect your progress.

Letting Go With Grace

Letting go doesn't mean dishonor. You can love people from a distance and release them without bitterness. Everyone has a place in your story—but not everyone has a place in every chapter.

**"Do not be misled: 'Bad company corrupts good character.'"
—1 Corinthians 15:33 (NIV)**

How to Know When It's Time to Separate

- You feel spiritually hindered when you're around them.

- Your values and vision no longer align.
- You can't take the next step until you lighten your load.
- God is stirring your heart to move in a different direction.

"Therefore, since we are surrounded by such a great cloud of witnesses, let us throw off everything that hinders and the sin that so easily entangles. And let us run with perseverance the race marked out for us." —Hebrews 12:1 (NIV)

Key Scriptures

- Genesis 12:1–4
- Genesis 13:9
- Amos 3:3
- 1 Corinthians 15:33
- Hebrews 12:1
- Matthew 14:22

Reflection Questions

1. Are there relationships or attachments that God is asking you to release?

2. Are you afraid to let go of what's familiar, even if it's holding you back?

3. How can you honor God by walking in obedience, even when it's lonely?

Declaration

I will not be held back by fear, familiarity, or misplaced loyalty. I release what no longer aligns with God's purpose for my life. I walk boldly through the door He has opened, trusting that He will bring the right people for the right season. I move forward with peace, focus, and grace.

Prayer

Lord, help me to discern who is called to walk with me into this next season. Give me the strength to release what hinders and the grace to walk in obedience, even when it's difficult. Align my relationships with Your will, and surround me with people who push me toward purpose. In Jesus' name. Amen.

Chapter 19

Seasons of Closed Doors Are Temporary

"See, I am doing a new thing! Now it springs up; do you not perceive it? I am making a way in the wilderness and streams in the wasteland." —Isaiah 43:19 (NIV)

Every Closed Door Has an Expiration Date

In your journey with God, closed doors are inevitable—but they are not permanent. Seasons of waiting, silence, or denial often feel final, but God uses them to shape, prepare, and redirect you for greater things. The God who shuts doors also knows when and how to open them again.

"There is a time for everything, and a season for every activity under the heavens:" —Ecclesiastes 3:1 (NIV)

The door may be shut today, but the season will shift. What seems like a dead end now could become your greatest testimony tomorrow.

Closed Doors Are Often Protective, Not Punitive

When God closes a door, He is not punishing you—He is often protecting you from something or preserving you for something better. Just because you don't understand it yet doesn't mean God isn't working behind the scenes.

**"And we know that in all things God works for the good of those who love him, who have been called according to his purpose."
—Romans 8:28 (NIV)**

Your job is not to pry open what He has closed, but to trust that He's making a new way in the wilderness.

Example: Jesus and Lazarus

When Lazarus died, it looked like the door of healing had closed. But Jesus had a greater plan: resurrection. What looked like a permanent loss became a platform for glory.

"Did I not tell you that if you believe, you will see the glory of God?" —John 11:40 (NIV)

Delay is not denial. Some closed doors are waiting to be reopened at the appointed time, for a greater purpose.

When Doors Close, Look for the New Thing

Isaiah 43:19 reminds us that even in wilderness places, God is creating something fresh. A closed door is often God's invitation to change your focus.

- **The job didn't work out**, but now you're discovering your calling.

- **The relationship ended**, but it made room for healing and growth.

- **The opportunity was denied**, but it forced you to depend on God more deeply.

"Forget the former things; do not dwell on the past." —Isaiah 43:18 (NIV)

Your assignment is not in the past—it's in what God is bringing forth next.

How to Endure Closed Door Seasons

1. Keep Seeking God's Presence

Don't disconnect just because things don't go your way.

"You will seek me and find me when you seek me with all your heart." —Jeremiah 29:13 (NIV)

2. Stay Faithful in the Waiting

Even when nothing moves, your obedience matters.

3. Expect the Unexpected

God doesn't just restore what was lost—He often gives better than what was denied.

"After Job had prayed for his friends, the Lord restored his fortunes and gave him twice as much as he had before." —Job 42:10 (NIV)

4. Write the Vision Again

What door are you believing God to open in the future? Start preparing like it's on the way.

Key Scriptures

- Isaiah 43:19
- Ecclesiastes 3:1
- Romans 8:28
- John 11:40
- Isaiah 43:18
- Jeremiah 29:13
- Job 42:10

Reflection Questions

1. Are you dwelling on a door God has already closed?

2. What "new thing" might God be trying to birth in your current season?

3. How can you remain faithful and expectant while you wait?

Declaration

Closed doors will not define me. I believe that every season of delay is preparing me for a greater door of destiny. I choose to trust God's timing, even when I don't understand it. I declare that this closed-door season is temporary, and new life is springing forth in Jesus' name.

Prayer

Father, thank You for being Lord over every door—open and closed. Help me not to be discouraged when things don't go as planned. Strengthen my heart to wait with hope, serve with faith, and expect with joy. I believe You are making a new way. Let me perceive it. In Jesus' name. Amen.

Chapter 20

God's Open Door Leads to Abundant Life

"The thief does not come except to steal, and to kill, and to destroy. I have come that they may have life, and that they may have it more abundantly." —John 10:10 (NKJV)

The Open Door is a Pathway to Fullness

God never opens a door just to give you access to more things—He opens it to give you access to more of Him, more of His purpose, more of His presence, and more of His promises. The ultimate goal of every divine door is not simply progress—it's abundant life in Christ.

"I am the door. If anyone enters by Me, he will be saved, and will go in and out and find pasture." —John 10:9 (NKJV)

Jesus is not just the One who opens doors—He is the Door. And when you walk through Him, you don't just find a better opportunity; you find a better life.

Abundant Life is Not Measured by Possessions

Abundance in Christ is not defined by wealth, status, or ease. It is defined by:

- Peace in the midst of pressure.

- Joy that doesn't depend on circumstances.
- Purpose that outlasts seasons.
- Strength that sustains through storms.
- Grace that empowers your walk.

The world offers counterfeit abundance—temporary highs that lead to empty places. But God's abundance is eternal and soul-deep.

"The blessing of the Lord makes one rich, and He adds no sorrow with it." —Proverbs 10:22 (NKJV)

The Door Leads to Purpose and Pasture

Jesus described the open door not just as salvation, but as a place of nourishment and rest.

"I am the door. If anyone enters by Me, he will be saved, and will go in and out and find pasture." —John 10:9 (NKJV)

Pasture speaks of:

- **Provision** – Your needs are met in Christ.

- **Peace** – You are not striving or chasing.

- **Freedom** – You are led, not driven.

God doesn't just want to open doors to busy you—He opens doors to bless you, grow you, and guide you into fruitful places.

Example: The Shepherd's Gate

In ancient times, the shepherd was the literal door to the sheepfold—lying down across the gate at night to protect the sheep. This is what Jesus meant: *"I am the door."*

When you enter through Christ, you don't just gain access—you gain protection, direction, and relationship.

How to Walk in Abundant Life Daily

- **Stay connected to the Source**

Abundance flows from Jesus, not from the door itself.

- **Abide in the Word**

"If you abide in Me, and My words abide in you, you will ask what you desire, and it shall be done for you." —John 15:7 (NKJV)

- **Prioritize spiritual fruit over material gain**

What's the condition of your heart, not just your harvest?

- **Remain thankful**

Gratitude multiplies joy and guards against discontentment.

- **Keep giving what you've received**

Abundance grows when it's shared through love, generosity, and service.

Key Scriptures

- John 10:9–10
- Proverbs 10:22
- John 15:7
- Philippians 4:19
- Psalm 23:1–2

Reflection Questions

1. Are you experiencing abundant life—or are you settling for survival?

2. What parts of your life need to realign with Jesus as the source?

3. How can you share the abundance you've received with others?

Declaration

I have entered the open door through Jesus Christ. I am no longer bound by fear, lack, or striving. I walk in peace, purpose, and provision. I declare that I am living the abundant life, not because of what I have, but because of who I have. My joy, strength, and identity are rooted in Him.

Prayer

Lord, thank You for being the Door and the Shepherd. I receive the abundant life You promised—peace, purpose, and joy in every season. Help me to walk daily in the fullness of Your Spirit, to trust You as my source, and to share what You've given with those around me. In You, I lack nothing. In Jesus' name. Amen.

Conclusion

The Door Is Open—Now Walk In!

"I know your works. See, I have set before you an open door, and no one can shut it…" —Revelation 3:8 (NKJV)

This Is Your Moment

You've stood at the threshold. You've heard the call. You've prayed, waited, prepared, and been refined. The time has come. The door is open—now walk in.

This book has walked you through 20 chapters of revelation, instruction, encouragement, and truth. You've seen how God opens doors with purpose, positions you for promotion, prepares you through waiting, and even strengthens you through closed doors. You've learned to discern the real from the counterfeit, and you've discovered that every open door is not about convenience—it's about kingdom assignment.

But now comes the most important part: responding.

God has not merely set the door before you to admire. He's asking you to trust Him enough to walk through it.

Not when it's comfortable.
Not when you feel qualified.
Not when others agree.
But now.

"...behold, now is the accepted time; behold, now is the day of salvation." —2 Corinthians 6:2 (KJV)

The Door Represents a Divine Invitation

When Jesus said, "I have set before you an open door," He was not just making a promise—He was issuing a divine summons. It's an invitation to step into:

- Greater faith.
- Greater obedience.
- Greater surrender.
- Greater purpose.

God doesn't just call the equipped—He equips the called. The door He has opened before you is proof that He has already gone ahead of you.

"And the Lord, he it is that doth go before thee; he will be with thee, he will not fail thee, neither forsake thee: fear not, neither be dismayed." —Deuteronomy 31:8 (KJV)

You're not walking into this alone. You're walking with heaven's backing.

Walking Through the Door May Cost You Something

Let's be honest—obedience often requires sacrifice. You may have to leave some people behind. You may need to let go of fear, pride, or comfort. You might need to start again. But hear this: *Whatever you leave behind cannot compare to what God is leading you into.*

"But as it is written, Eye hath not seen, nor ear heard, neither have entered into the heart of man, the things which God hath prepared for them that love him." —1 Corinthians 2:9 (KJV)

What Awaits on the Other Side?

- Peace that surpasses understanding.
- Purpose that gives life meaning.
- Joy that no storm can steal.
- Fruit that multiplies beyond your imagination.
- Influence that advances God's kingdom.
- Restoration in areas you thought were forever broken.

This is not just about a new opportunity—this is about stepping into your God-ordained destiny.

A Final Challenge: Don't Just Read—Respond

Books can inspire, but only decisions activate transformation. God has placed something in your hands. Maybe it's a ministry, message, mission, business, calling, burden, or a promise. And the door is open.

Will you walk through?

This isn't the end. This is the beginning of a new chapter in your life. One marked by boldness, humility, integrity, and faithfulness. A chapter where you stop second-guessing and start saying yes to the God who has already gone before you.

"Ye have not chosen me, but I have chosen you, and ordained you, that ye should go and bring forth fruit, and that your fruit

should remain: that whatsoever ye shall ask of the Father in my name, he may give it you." —John 15:16 (KJV)

Reflection Questions

1. What open door is God placing before you right now?

2. What is holding you back from stepping through it?

3. What first step of faith can you take today?

Declaration

The door is open, and I will walk in. I will not be held back by fear, doubt, or delay. I trust the One who opened the door before me. I declare that this is my season of divine movement, kingdom impact, and supernatural fulfillment. I walk forward boldly, by faith, and for His glory.

Prayer

Father, thank You for every door You've opened, every lesson You've taught, and every season You've sustained me through. I choose to respond in faith. I walk through the door You have set before me with courage, obedience, and trust. Let my life bear lasting fruit for Your kingdom. Use me for Your glory, and lead me every step of the way. In Jesus' name. Amen.

Scripture Index by Theme

Open Doors and Divine Access

- Revelation 3:7–8
- Isaiah 22:22
- Colossians 4:3
- 1 Corinthians 16:9
- 2 Corinthians 2:12
- John 10:9

Faith and Obedience

- Hebrews 11:1, 8
- 2 Corinthians 5:7
- Romans 1:17
- James 2:17, 26
- Matthew 7:7

Fear and Courage

- 2 Timothy 1:7
- Joshua 1:9
- Isaiah 41:10
- Psalm 27:1

Waiting and Timing

- Ecclesiastes 3:1
- Habakkuk 2:3

- Isaiah 40:31
- Lamentations 3:26
- Psalm 27:14

Character and Integrity

- Proverbs 11:3
- Proverbs 10:9
- Psalm 51:10
- Luke 16:10
- 1 Corinthians 4:2

Purpose and Promotion

- Proverbs 18:16
- Esther 4:14
- 1 Peter 5:6
- John 15:16
- Matthew 25:21

Discernment and Wisdom

- Proverbs 3:5–6
- Matthew 7:15–20
- 1 John 4:1
- Amos 3:3
- Philippians 1:9–10

Prayer and Power

- Colossians 4:2–3
- James 5:16

- Daniel 10:12
- Luke 18:1–8
- Jeremiah 33:3

www.ingramcontent.com/pod-product-compliance
Lightning Source LLC
LaVergne TN
LVHW022317080426
835509LV00036B/2515